Winter in the LAKE DISTRICT

Winter in the
LAKE DISTRICT

Contents

HALF-TITLE PAGE A February day on Derwentwater.

TITLE PAGE Wide pools along the River Brathay as it leaves Elterwater.

LEFT Cloud rolling around Brotherswater and the Patterdale valley.

Preface

If I have one complaint about winter in the Lake District it is that it isn't cold enough, 2010 excepted! Cold and frosty weather is often bright and sunny too, and though there are many who don't enjoy this weather, I just love it. I don't mind how cold it gets; I covet those crisp days of clear skies and no wind. This to me is perfect Lake District winter weather, better even than a fall of snow, and if it would only stay this way for weeks on end I would never want to go away. Freezing nights can be wonderful too. It is fairly easy to get well away from lights, wrap up warm and gaze at the heavens filled with stars. And the sight of a full moon rising over the surface of a still dark lake is unforgettable.

Cumbrian people are always divided on the question of snow. There are those who love it, and those who hate it. The weather forecasters always talk about snow as 'bad' weather. Many of us wouldn't agree. I'm certain most photographers wouldn't – it's a golden opportunity to go out and get winter photos, provided the roads have been cleared. There used to be more of it, unless that's just my imagination playing tricks. We treasure the memory of a row of skis outside the local pub as we moved into our house just before Christmas twenty-five years ago – being skiing enthusiasts we really felt we had come to the right place. As I remember, there were many occasions in those early years when I was able to ski locally on my cross-country pair for several days on end. Sadly, though, those dazzling days of white snow and blue skies are now a rarity. These winters the snow may fall on the mountains, but rarely to valley level. More often the weather stays windy and grey.

However, even our more typical winter weather can have its compensations. I hate wind, but have to admit that the transient ever-shifting light on a windy day makes the Lake District an exceptionally rewarding place to photograph. Unsettled conditions can lead to wonderful effects, as cloud scuds across the fells, breaking to allow shafts of sunshine that light up little scenes on the valley floor.

My favourite light, comes on those gorgeous mornings when banks of mist slowly drift and clear above the lakes and valleys to disclose vistas reminiscent of Japanese watercolours. Or, best of all, and more common in winter, are those magnificent moments of inversion, when it is possible to climb above the cloud and see mountain after mountain summit peeking out above a fluffy white mantle.

I have particularly enjoyed working on this book. It took me to so many wonderful places in the quieter months of the year. My only problem was trying to choose which photographs to include. It was so hard – I'd ended up with far too much material. But I think the final selection shows why I'm such an advocate of winter in the Lake District.

Val Corbett

RIGHT The snow-clad slopes around Brotherswater were lit by the full moon on this bitterly cold but extraordinarily beautiful night. Orion's Belt can be seen in the night sky, and the lights of the Brotherswater Inn are reflected in the lake.

6

The onset of winter

There is usually a magic little interlude – before the final battering gales of autumn blast the last leaves off the trees – of wonderful late autumn light when the colours are so strong that they tend towards the surreal. The intense green of the valley floors makes a dramatic contrast with the gold of the dying bracken, the colours becoming yet more concentrated after rain. Softer days with mists and hazy sunshine come almost as a welcome relief.

The first proper snow on the fell tops generally falls somewhere around the middle of November. We like to gather a late harvest of fungi such as chanterelles. Sloes, softened by the first frosts are now ready for picking, soon to be made into sloe gin. The last of the autumn sheep shows, at Buttermere in mid October, signals the end of another season.

LEFT These fallen autumn leaves on Askham village green looked wonderful when rimed with frost. It was a real sign of the turning of the seasons.

FOLLOWING PAGE Late autumn at Loughrigg Tarn. The early days of November are my very favourite time for taking landscape photos. My busy summer schedule photographing gardens is well and truly over. Half term has come and gone and the Lake District finally becomes quieter. Most years there is still plenty of autumn colour.

RIGHT A red squirrel on our lawn busily stowing away nuts. In this instance the nuts were conkers that I had collected together to photograph, but the squirrel had other ideas. We had 'reds' in abundance a few years ago and spent many happy hours watching their antics. A memorable sight was one trying to run along the washing line, but getting confounded by the clothes pegs. Nowadays we feel honoured that we still get the occasional visitor, and are aware that their days in our valley are probably numbered. They will be sorely missed.

LEFT The little knot of yews, protected by a sturdy wall, shelters the tiny church of St Olaf, with its gravestones telling of the early mountaineers who lost their lives in the surrounding mountains. The light dusting of new snow on the summit of Great Gable was the very first of that winter. A plaque on the rocky outcrop that forms the summit cairn commemorates members of the Fell and Rock Climbing Club who lost their lives in the First World War. Following the short ceremony on Remembrance Sunday, simple wreaths and poppy crosses are laid around. The plaque was dedicated in 1924, the club having purchased land that included Great Gable and donated it to the National Trust in memory of those fallen members.

RIGHT These Swaledale sheep have been rounded up onto pastures below Blencathra, where the first snows of winter can be seen on the summit. Typically in mid-November there are still some burnished leaves on the oaks. Those who enjoy winter relish its onset, with the first sight of snow. Personally I'm happy to see the snow but it's the darker nights and grey, wet and windy weather I can do without.

BELOW The gather of the sheep from the high fells is a sure sign that winter is on its way – shepherds don't like to leave it until there is a chance of heavy snow. These Herdwick sheep, crossing the packhorse bridge at Wasdale Head, were going to lower pastures in the less mountainous parts of Cumbria. Others would be going to the large sheep markets held at this time of the year.

LEFT A late autumn morning looking across mist-filled Derwentwater to Cat Bells and the fells surrounding Newlands Valley. My viewpoint was Castlehead, a short sharp climb above Keswick, with a magnificent view in almost every direction.

The mountains and high passes

'Is the Lake District large or small?' This is a question I often use as a time filler – a distraction – as I'm puffing up some fell. Of course the answer is, 'it's small'. Stand on one of many mountain summits near the boundary of the Lake District and it's possible to see peaks on the furthest side. But then again the answer is, 'it's large'. And the truth is that the huge variety in the scenery makes the area feel far larger than it really is. The mountains in particular display their varied geological histories, so that, for example, the stately rounded slate dome of Skiddaw is distinctly different from the knobbly Borrowdale volcanics of the Langdale Pikes. The peaks are distinctive with recognisable profiles. On any mountain summit you can hear some man identifying them all at the top of his voice. (As a rule of thumb, the louder the voice, the more they get wrong.)

In winter the mountains are uniquely beautiful, with a distinctly 'Lake District' look that I believe to be unlike that of any other area, either in Britain – or indeed – the world. When the clouds clear, the sharper, lower light of winter shows them at their very best. They are also at their most colourful, their slopes vivid with rust-coloured bracken and their summits frequently white with dustings of snow. Later, on the highest mountains, spectacular cornices gradually build up.

RIGHT The view from Newlands Pass across Sail Beck to the dark screes and colourful bracken slopes of Eel Crag (also known as Crag Hill), Sail and Causey Pike.

ABOVE The simple shapes looking towards the massive western slopes of Blencathra from Latrigg make striking abstract shapes when seen in winter. In summer the bracken in the middle band will be green and the contrast far less arresting. In general, the cleaner, more graphic outlines of the landscape in winter are helpful for achieving eye-catching compositions.

BELOW Rowan trees, often known as mountain ash, grow surprisingly high up on the mountain slopes and in ghylls. Traditionally they were planted outside houses to ward off evil, but I've also read the same story about holly and hawthorn. Although I love their bare branches in winter, they are best seen in early autumn when they are resplendent with clusters of red berries. The berries can be made into jellies, though it's wise to collect them when you see them – the birds can strip the whole lot overnight.

FOLLOWING PAGE The slopes of Red Screes and Caudale frame the view when looking north from Kirkstone Pass. Some parts of the pass are extremely steep and one section in particular, known as The Struggle, leaving Ambleside, can prove quite a challenge for drivers. In earlier times of horse-drawn carriages, passengers were required to get out and walk. As with other Lake District passes, the weather can be surprisingly different on one side compared with the other.

ABOVE Two Herdwick sheep take a brief pause from their endless cropping of the short winter grasses on the mountain summit. Many Lakeland sheep are brought down to the lower pastures of the Eden Valley or Cumbrian coastal plain but the Herdwick is a particularly tough breed – if trapped in snowdrifts they may actually eat their own fleece, the fatty lanolin providing them with a survival aid. Herdwick sheep are native to Cumbria and Beatrix Potter was a knowledgeable breeder, judging at sheep fairs and leaving the National Trust a huge acreage of land and her flock of sheep on her death.

OPPOSITE TOP A little late season fresh snow mingles with earlier snow near the summit of Helvellyn, looking across Swirral Edge to Raise and the Dodds, with Blencathra and Skiddaw in the far distance.

OPPOSITE BOTTOM The iconic view of Wasdale with Great Gable flanked by Yewbarrow and Lingmell was voted 'Britain's Favourite View' in 2008. The National Park has based its logo on precisely this view. The superlatives extend: Scafell Pike, just off on the right, is England's highest mountain whilst Wastwater is its deepest lake.

ABOVE The wall leading to the summit of High Street is close to the line of the old Roman road of the same name. That road ran for twenty-eight miles from Brougham Fort, near Penrith, to Galava at Ambleside. A connecting Roman road then ran westwards, over Hardknott Pass, to the strategic port of Ravenglass on the Cumbrian coast. Although exposed to the weather, routes along the bare mountain tops were preferable to the forested valleys. High Street was previously known as Racecourse Hill as its summit plateau was used in earlier times for horse racing.

BELOW The old A66 runs parallel
to the modern trunk road and I
sometimes choose to drive that
way, dodging the potholes, so
I can enjoy the onward views of
Blencathra at my own pace.

RIGHT Ill Bell, one of the summits
of the Kentmere Horseshoe, towers
above Troutbeck Park.

RIGHT The mountain of Blencathra on a gloriously sunny alpine day following heavy snowfall. Deep snow and blue sky is a combination that sadly has become only too rare. To my mind, Blencathra is the best looking of the Lakeland mountains. Sharp Edge, originally known as 'Razor Edge' is in sunlight on the far right and is notorious for a dangerous awkward step. The Keswick Mountain Rescue Team answers regular call-outs to incidents where people have fallen or become cragfast. Ten fatalities have been logged but the greasiness of the worn slate means that by no means all the falls are due to winter conditions.

LEFT A Christmas Day walk with my family brought us to the vantage point of Heughscar overlooking Ullswater to Place Fell and the Helvellyn range. The weather was great but cold and we were lucky to bump into old friends who shared with us their large flask of well-laced mulled wine.

BELOW Rays of golden light from the setting sun catch the highest ridges on Causey Pike and Crag Hill. Derwentwater, below, is in shadow, its frozen surface coated with snow and cut through with darker cracks in the ice.

ABOVE Although the road over Kirkstone Pass was cleared of snow, the drifts against the walls on either side of the road were reminders of the earlier blizzard conditions. The outcome of the high winds can be seen in the sculpturing of the snow and, in the far distance, the wind has in places blown snow off the slopes of the Troutbeck Fells, Yoke, Froswick and Ill Bell.

The valleys

One of the things I most love about the Lake District is the way each valley has its own distinctive character and how people love arguing about which is the best. Geology is part of the reason – compare, for example, the wide U shape of Great Langdale, produced by ice age action, with the steep-sided water-eroded valley of Coledale near Keswick. Building stone varies from valley to valley; the walls and buildings of one valley are often identifiably different from those of its neighbour just across the fell.

The industrial heritage differs too – for instance, many signs remain of copper mining in Coniston, former (and present-day) slate quarrying in Little Langdale and early gold and lead mining in the remote valleys of the northern fells.

In winter the southern valleys, facing the low winter sun, can be as warm as toast and perfect for winter walks on sunny days. It's worth doing a bit of shrewd planning to devise a mid-winter walk in day-long sunshine.

ABOVE The magnificent flat-bottomed valley of Great Langdale, with its covering of snow acting as a reminder of its formation in the ice age.

LEFT Dramatic mountains dwarf the little hamlet of Wasdale Head. Generations of climbers have stayed at the Wasdale Head Inn while doing the classic climbs on Great Gable, Pillar and Scafell. Today it has its own microbrewery and each winter hosts the annual 'World's Biggest Liar' competition, when entrants get five minutes to tell a tall story. The rules stipulate that 'politicians and lawyers are excluded from entry'.

BELOW I have sentimental attachments to this double-arched bridge at Grange in Borrowdale. My father, in the 1920s (and in his 20s), made an amateur cine film with a gang of friends, which involved a lovelorn suitor throwing his rival off the bridge. In addition, on my first visit to the Lakes as a child, we spent a holiday in a slate-clad guesthouse overlooking the bridge. And yes, it rained every day.

RIGHT Lorton is a wonderful valley, the gateway from the west to some of the Lake District's most inspirational scenery. After the attractive villages of Low and High Lorton, the road splits near this farmhouse, going to Crummock Water and Buttermere in one direction and Loweswater in another.

ABOVE The small village of Patterdale lies snugly beneath the Helvellyn range. The normal route up from Patterdale via Grisedale leads up to the Hole in the Wall on the prominent snowy ridge. The route then traverses the challenging Striding Edge and ascends steeply (as seen on page 72) to the summit plateau. Every winter's day, the National Park's Fell-top Assessors visit the summit to record conditions underfoot and the weather and then make them available by phone or internet. The public make half a million internet requests each year.

RIGHT The view from the lower slopes of Place Fell across the head of Ullswater. The village of Glenridding and the Greenside Valley are on the far shore of the lake along with the steamer piers from which sailings are made throughout the year.

RIGHT Low cloud over the eastern fells of the Lake District near Shap lifts just enough to allow shafts of sunshine to illuminate patches of distant fellside and these snow-covered fields. The stone walls make contrasting angular patterns.

RIGHT Sheep are given supplementary feed throughout the winter using the previous summer's hay crop. Fell sheep, such as these in Langdale, are 'heafed', that is they instinctively stay close to their place of suckling, making a farmer's life far simpler.

BELOW Little Town, nestling under the slopes of Cat Bells in the Newlands Valley, was the setting for Beatrix Potter's *Mrs Tiggiwinkle*. When our children were very young we would often walk up Cat Bells. On one occasion I sneaked ahead to a small cave and hid a toy Mrs Tiggiwinkle, along with a miniature ironing board and basket of clothes, for the girls to 'discover'. However, I think we were well and truly rumbled.

ABOVE Sheep leave the shelter of the stone walls and crowd around the feeder on this bitter day. Others patiently scrape away in the snow to find small patches of grass.

LEFT A juvenile stag (red deer) in snow.

OPPOSITE TOP The village of Patterdale gets some winter sun. It lies at the foot of the deeply cut valley of Grisedale, the floor of which, in contrast, sees no sun for most of the winter months.

OPPOSITE LEFT Martindale, seen from Hallin Fell. The mountain at the far right, The Nab, is home to a herd of red deer, which have been reported as the only pure-blooded red deer left in England. In winter the herd will come down to the fields for feeding.

OPPOSITE RIGHT Blea Tarn House in Langdale is genuinely isolated in a way that few houses in the Lake District valleys are. The attached barn is now home to the Lancashire Mountaineering Club. Side Pike, rising steeply behind the house, has one of the best views of the Great Langdale Valley.

ABOVE St Michael's Church stands on a wonderful site, where a church has existed for 1000 years or so. Perched above the River Lowther on one side and beside Lowther Park on the other, the present church dates from 1686. Inside there are splendid marble memorials to members of the Lowther family and a mausoleum lies within the churchyard. The park is a listed landscape with wonderful avenues of oaks and the romantic ruin of Lowther Castle.

RIGHT Our neighbour's traditional stone Lakeland cottage lies snug beneath a coat of heavy snow.

BELOW A wintry dawn over Knipe Scar and the Lowther Valley on the eastern fringe of the Lake District.

ABOVE This track passes St Olaf's church on its way to Burnthwaite, the National Trust farm at the head of Wasdale. It then splits, the left fork is to Beck Head, the pass seen here between Kirk Fell on the left and Great Gable, while the other is the popular route to Sty Head Pass.

ABOVE Evening sun illuminates the
far end of the Grisedale Valley.

ABOVE Blowing snow has coated these dry stone walls in the Lowther Valley.

LEFT The particularly attractive village of Askham, near Ullswater, has an unusually long and wide village green, lined with traditional cottages, many of which date from the seventeenth century. That period of peace, after the ending of the Border raids, saw a rapid growth in the building of stone cottages in many Lake District villages. Previously, stone buildings usually included defensive pele towers to protect the population, whilst smaller houses were of wooden construction.

BELOW The Mill House by the River Lowther at Askham is just brilliantly situated. Floods often threaten it, to recede just before they inundate the ground floor. The red painted lintels stand out on this snowy day.

ABOVE AND LEFT No one knows for certain the origins of the large circle of standing stones at Castlerigg above the valley of St John's in the Vale, but the thousands of visitors who come year round determinedly photograph each other against various stones. These may well make an interesting archive in centuries to come. My most memorable experience happened early one stunningly beautiful morning. A traveller emerged from her exotic caravan with a conch shell. She stood at the centre of the circle and blew haunting tones into the vast stillness. It was quite simply too inspiring a moment to spoil by clicking a camera shutter.

LEFT The view across Newlands Valley from Cat Bells, one late November evening.

RIGHT Bridge End is one of several lovely traditional Lakeland farmhouses owned by the National Trust in the valley of Little Langdale. Some remain as part of working farms while others are now let for holiday accommodation.

BELOW There always has to be one, doesn't there? But here there are two. These Herdwick sheep at Wall End in Great Langdale have clambered out of the barn to play 'King of the Castle' on their bales of winter feed. The barn itself is sturdy enough, and a work of art being built of dry stone without so much as a trace of cement.

LEFT A rainstorm passing
briefly over the valley head of
Martindale. Swiftly changing
light and weather is so
characteristic of the Lakes and
one of the joys of photography
– provided you've got a
waterproof handy.

ABOVE Rays of sun illuminate fields in St John's in the Vale, as the Helvellyn mountain range looms threateningly above.

RIGHT Newlands – the December sun setting behind Robinson. Valleys going into deep shadow can be a problem in winter photography, but sometimes it all works out for the best.

RIGHT In previous centuries the now tranquil valley of Greenside, above Glenridding, was a busy industrial area with a highly successful lead mine. Although the mine was the first in the country to have electric light (hydroelectricity from the dam at Keppel Cove), walking to and from the levels high on the mountainside on dark winter mornings and evenings must have been tough.

BELOW The profile of the Langdale Pikes is almost certainly the best known mountain shape in Britain. This wonderful view is from the roadside – no wonder it is photographed so often. The Herdwick sheep are generally brought down from the higher fells for over-wintering.

A day of inversion

Winter in the Lake District can drag on, with a seemingly endless diet of dreary wet and windy weather. And then a day of such staggering beauty comes along, that all is forgiven and thoughts of heading south for the sun go on to the back-burner again. One such recent occasion was New Year's Eve, when most of the area was experiencing a bitterly cold day of Stygian gloom. However, just above the height of Kirkstone Pass, on the path to Red Screes, a different world existed. There was warm sunshine with stunning views over cloud-filled valleys with a host of mountain summits peeking above the murk. Inversion almost certainly happens without my knowing it – I have often thought that web cams on mountain summits would be helpful – but this day surpassed any other I have experienced.

LEFT The lights of Kirkstone Pass Inn
guide my way home that evening.

ABOVE Mickledore, the cleft between
Scafell and Scafell Pike is clearly
outlined on the horizon.

ABOVE Looking west, late in the afternoon, to Hardknott Pass with Harter Fell in the fold behind.

Winter activities

It's a well known fact that the Lake District experiences the highest rainfall in England – sometimes it feels like the highest in the world. One of winter's most depressing sights is a row of sodden sheep attempting to shelter in the lee of a dry stone wall.

However, despite the climate, life does exist in the Lake District in winter. And some of it even happens outdoors. When there really is no relief from the rain, it's best to head for one of the Lake District's cosy pubs and hang out by a fire. There are several micro-breweries operating from pubs in the Lake District – dodge a walk and opt for another variety of Cumbrian wetness. Domino drives and quizzes are common on winter nights in the pubs. Choirs, evening classes and a multitude of societies abound. Keswick and Kendal are well known not just as tourist centres but also for their literature and film festivals. The Kendal Mountain Film Festival takes place appropriately in November. An increasing number of the large houses and castles now stay open throughout the winter and encourage visitors by hosting events – Muncaster Castle has a Halloween week, Dalemain a Marmalade Festival.

Hopes for a white Christmas are seldom realised but the area teems with visitors at Christmas and New Year. Food preparations start early, with local specialities such as Cumberland sauce, Cumberland rum butter and damson gin adding a Cumbrian character to the feast. The large hotels mark New Year's Eve with a firework display – a particularly wonderful sight when reflected in a lake.

And then there's outdoor fun. Many walkers eagerly wait for the moment when high-level snow consolidates and they can start strapping on their crampons. A reliable snow field on a north-facing slope, high on the side of Raise, near Helvellyn, is used by the Lake District Ski Club, which runs a button lift. Ski mountaineers carry their equipment to the summits and manage incredible descents of derring-do. More and more cross-country skiers are also to be seen.

LEFT The various bodies that might have responsibility for rescue generally frown upon skating on the larger lakes. However, the smaller shallower tarns freeze across and might be considered a safe bet in exceptionally frosty conditions.

RIGHT This wonderful spiral, created by boot prints on the frozen surface of Derwentwater, was cleverly done. I was curious about its origin and found out by chance many months later that the manager of the Youth Hostel close by was responsible.

LEFT The hard packed snow transformed Crow Park in Keswick into a perfect tobogganing slope.

BELOW Most local schools were closed following this unusually heavy snowfall. It didn't take long for friends to get together and go sledging, as here at Askham in the Lowther Valley.

ABOVE These three jolly snowmen greeted walkers on the path down from Walla Crag.

RIGHT My younger daughter, Roz, gets busy making a snowman, though it ended up as a voluptuous snowwoman.

FOLLOWING PAGE Wrapping up warm and getting out on a boat trip is a great way to see the Lakes in winter, so much better than sitting in the car. The larger lakes of Windermere, Derwentwater and Ullswater nowadays benefit from year-round boat services. Interesting linear walks are made possible by hopping off at any one of the landing stages. Santa comes on board around Christmas time with presents for the children and sherry and mince pies for the adults.

LEFT A welcome hot drink on a cold but beautiful walk, near the summit of Place Fell. Brotherswater, with Kirkstone Pass and Red Screes beyond, is in the far distance.

BELOW A group of schoochildren on Matterdale Common having a lesson unusual in England – learning to ski.

TOP LEFT A climber, with his skis strapped to his back, climbs the final steep section above Red Tarn to the summit of Helvellyn. I've come up an easy route and can only stand and watch in awe.

TOP RIGHT Little Hell Gate, the only sensible route (for walkers rather than climbers) on Great Gable's west face, leads directly to the summit. Classic climbing routes are all around, with Napes Needle close at hand. The view over Wasdale arguably ranks as the best in the Lake District.

LEFT Racehorses from the Greystoke stables are occasionally exercised on Moordivock. The Helvellyn range and Ullswater can be seen in the far distance.

ABOVE The master of the Coniston
Foxhounds leaving Troutbeck.
In the Lake District, the hounds
are followed on foot rather than
on horse.

RIGHT Foxhounds arriving in their
trailer get an early sniff of what
is to come, but number three –
the poser! – already has its eye
on the camera.

RIGHT AND BELOW Pancake Day races in Troutbeck. In the men's event, two of the local chefs seem to have an edge over the vicar. Pupils from Windermere Junior School were having a lot more fun tossing the pancake than preparing for their SATs.

ABOVE Christmas shopping in
Keswick. The original Moot Hall
(meeting place) had a long history
of uses including a courthouse, a
prison and a butter market. The
rebuilt version of 1813 is now used
as a Tourist Information Centre.

LEFT Christmas shopping in Kendal.
The imposing round chimneystack
is typical of the area.

LEFT This sweet shop, in Kirkby Lonsdale, always looks a treat, but particularly so when it's decorated for Christmas.

RIGHT A Christmas shop window in Branthwaite Brow, a lovely old steep cobbled street in Kendal.

BOTTOM LEFT A Christmas tree in my local village.

BOTTOM RIGHT Traditional Grasmere Gingerbread is made in this pretty little shop, right by the lychgate to Grasmere church. A word of warning though – the wonderful spicy aroma as it is baking wafts into the street and is irresistible, especially on a cold winter's day.

The lakes, tarns, rivers and waterfalls

Nobody is going to deny that we get a lot of rain in the Lake District. Indeed Seathwaite, at the top end of Borrowdale, wins the trophy for being the wettest spot in England. But then we also have the most lakes, the longest lake, the deepest lake and without any doubt (several contenders here!) the most beautiful lake.

In settled winter weather, the mirror reflections of the surrounding mountains create the most glorious images. After several days of proper frost, a wide rim of ice fringes the shallower bays of the lakes, while the small tarns freeze over. Streams and waterfalls are silent, with a wonderful array of ice sculptures created by the drips and splashings of any remaining running water.

But on a thoroughly wet day there is nothing better than to don rain gear and wellies and go off to gaze at the thundering waterfalls. The saturated fells become streaked with white ribbons of water, cascading streams overflow their beds and springs suddenly bubble up out of nowhere.

RIGHT The angular profile of Fleetwith Pike is reflected in Buttermere.

LEFT This treasured view of a picture-perfect row of Scots pines on the shore of Buttermere is one of the most frequently photographed and painted scenes in the Lake District.

BOTTOM LEFT The same scene but on a completely different day. On this chilly occasion, the early mist shrouded High Crag, which was slowly revealed only as the sun burnt through and the mist lifted. I rather enjoy the unusual atmosphere of this simple shot.

BELOW Unlike the relatively flat northern end of Ullswater, the southern end of the lake is characterised by the crowding-in mountains, with steep slopes on all sides. For this reason, Glenridding and Patterdale are popular with walkers, and a fine winter's day will see crowds heading off in every direction to enjoy the fells. The steep foot of Place Fell, on the east side of the lake, can be seen in the photograph.

RIGHT A winter dawn over Derwentwater, looking towards the Jaws of Borrowdale, with the snow sprinkled mountains of Glaramara and Great End in the far distance.

BELOW A man working in an Ambleside bakery brings the day's leftovers down to the lake to feed the swans and ducks on a bitterly cold December evening.

BELOW LEFT Walking down from Red Screes towards Ambleside in gathering darkness on a midwinter's evening can be a lovely experience, as the lights of the village in the valley below gradually start to shine. However, this evening the setting sun provided a wonderful glow across the gathering mist.

BELOW RIGHT The rosy pink of dawn on the Langdale Pikes, with Windermere in the foreground.

BELOW The Wastwater Screes, which form a formidable mile-and-a-half wall along the south shore of Wastwater, are seen at their best when a sprinkling of snow brings their dark and dramatic slopes into relief.

TOP The Duke of Portland boathouse at the northern end of Ullswater is a very popular subject for photographers.

MIDDLE On this, a blustery day, the biting winds had blown little scuds of slushy ice across Blea Tarn.

BOTTOM The boat landings at Keswick were temporarily out of service, the shallow water in the bay being frozen over.

TOP Tarn Hows is generally considered to be a beauty spot but I have my reservations about the close-in views.

MIDDLE The River Brathay leaves Elterwater and meanders peacefully through meadowland, forming a series of wide pools.

BOTTOM Evening light bathes this view across the frosty meadows to Coniston Lake.

ABOVE A popular short fell walk from Ambleside follows one bank of the Scandale Beck before crossing High Sweden Bridge, an ancient packhorse bridge, and returns on the opposite bank. Using packhorses was particularly suited to mountainous areas and Kendal was an important trading centre. In common with other narrow bridges, High Sweden was built without walls so as to avoid the panniers getting caught as the horse crossed.

LEFT After several nights of sharp frosts, ice builds up around the waterfall at Aira Force, near Ullswater. Unfortunately the frozen spray also builds up on the adjacent paths. Despite the hostile environment, a dipper continued to fly in and out of the rocky crevices amongst the icy sides.

ABOVE Easdale Tarn, high
above the Grasmere valley,
is set in a magnificent stadium
of mountains.

BELOW Torrential rain falling on frozen ground caused the level of Ullswater to rise dramatically. Substantial parts of Jenkin Field at Glenridding, an area normally enjoyed by the public, disappeared under water, leaving its benches marooned. Elsewhere along the lake shore, water flooded across the bordering roads, so that road and lake were indistinguishable – an alarming experience for any drivers.

RIGHT Days of driving rain and strong winds are, of course, not unknown in the Lake District. As is often said, those lakes have to get their water from somewhere. However, outside the very centre of the National Park and in particular at the valley heads, the rainfall figures are not exceptional. And my own view is that I would prefer to spend time on a very wet day getting out into the hills, well clad in waterproof gear, than shopping in any town. Here, a visitor braves it out on the end of the pier at Pooley Bridge.

BELOW The angular shapes of Fleetwith Pike, Haystacks and High Stile are reflected in Buttermere early on an intensely cold January morning. I was the solitary person on the silent lake shore, an area that is normally popular with walkers. Sometimes the sense of wonder at being quite alone in one of the most beautiful areas of the world can be quite overwhelming.

RIGHT This little group of rocks, near Friar's Crag on Derwentwater, is relatively boring if connected to the shore when the water level is lower in the summer. However, when the lake level is high, I love the way the rocky 'summits' remain above the water and an island is created which mimics the far skyline in its shape.

TOP LEFT An early morning in midwinter on Windermere. The lake will get quite busy later in the morning, with the coming and going of launches to the landing stage at Waterhead.

LEFT The busy Kirkstone Pass road passes just above the east shore of Brotherswater but tucked just out of sight are a series of surprisingly peaceful little bays.

ABOVE The mountains rise steeply around the southern end of Ullswater. Kirkstone Pass, the route to the south, is bathed in sunlight in the far distance.

ABOVE Haweswater generally looks better in the winter when the rainfall is higher. The reservoir supplies Manchester by gravity alone and the water level drops significantly during dry spells, exposing an unsightly rubble edge. On rare occasions the level drops sufficiently to expose the remains of the drowned village of Mardale. The ruined shepherds' huts in the foreground are on the Old Corpse Road, a track that linked Mardale to Shap. Coffins were transported on sleds or on the backs of packhorses.

FOLLOWING PAGE On this early January morning the bracken-covered slope of Cat Bells, in the foreground, is the colour of fresh rust. The Skiddaw massif and Blencathra are in the far distance, together forming a magnificent backdrop to Derwentwater.

LEFT The mountain of Melbreak forms a stern and massive wall above the west shore of Crummock Water. Climbing the mountain is steep from any direction until the surprisingly level large plateau is reached, which then sports two summits of almost equal height.

BELOW Swans stay year round in the Lakes and on Rydal will silently swim across to see whether they can cadge any food from visitors. Nab Cottage, on the far shore, has literary connections, being for a while the home of De Quincey. Coleridge was lodging here when he died.

TOP RIGHT The Langdale Pikes seem to have the knack of making excellent photogenic backdrops, whether on land or water. Their reflected profiles can be seen in Blea Tarn, Elterwater, Lake Windermere and, as here, in Loughrigg Tarn. Snow has coated the distant summits of Bow Fell and Crinkle Crags.

BOTTOM RIGHT A wonderful early February morning on Windermere, warm enough for the passengers on this launch to stay out on deck. The launches run right through the winter and a boat trip is often the first experience of visitors to the Lakes. It is without doubt a better experience than driving along the noisy and busy A591 along the east shore of the lake.

RIGHT Near the end of a perfect winter's day, with billowing clouds above fresh snow on the tops. The view across Brotherswater is to the steep slopes of Gray Crag with the High Street range in the far distance. Hartsop, a delightfully unspoilt hamlet, is on the far side of the lake.

FAR LEFT Frosted grasses form a delicate frame for this photo of the Coniston Fells reflected in the River Brathay.

ABOVE Soaring Scots pines frame the view over Glenridding and Ullswater from Keldas.

LEFT Evening sun, following an earlier fall of snow, illuminates Grasmoor, Whiteless Pike and Robinson. Loweswater (in the foreground) and Crummock Water are particularly peaceful lakes.

ABOVE One of the deep wide pools on the River Brathay shortly after leaving Elterwater meanders peacefully through meadowland, forming a series of wide pools, which appear to be beautiful little lakes. You have to be quick off the mark to take photos of deep snow, such as here, at valley level. Snow at such low levels is unusual in the Lake District and it tends to disappear within hours.

LEFT Dramatic late afternoon light on an almost flat calm Bassenthwaite Lake gives a reflection of the ridge of Ullock Pike, an attractive route to the snow-capped Skiddaw behind.

ABOVE The gradual path leading to the summit of Arthur's Pike from the north, along the route of the old Roman road of High Street, is a good choice in winter conditions for anyone not keen on tackling anything steep in snow or ice. However, the view from the summit cairn is disappointing. There is a far better viewpoint that is easy to miss from a large cairn less than a hundred metres down the mountain on the west. From this lower point the land drops away dramatically to allow this wonderfully unobstructed view of Ullswater.

ABOVE Mist rises from Ullswater on a frosty January morning.

TOP RIGHT On this bleak December day snow storms were sweeping across Mardale at the head of Haweswater. In the brief periods between the whiteouts, glimpses of the lake were revealed. The old village of Mardale, which was flooded in 1935 by the creation of Haweswater Reservoir, lies deep beneath the dark waters.

BOTTOM RIGHT Climb the fell of Gowbarrow, leaving Aira Force and its crowds behind, and you are quickly rewarded with glorious views of Ullswater. As you gain height the great corries and ridges of the Helvellyn range come into view. Lyulph's Tower in the foreground is an old hunting lodge built by the Howard family of Greystoke Castle.

BELOW Looking across Brotherswater to Hartsop Dodd and Caudale Moor. Kirkstone Pass, the lowest point on the right, was blocked – I know, I tried it!

ABOVE Kidsty Pike, heavily blanketed with snow, is reflected in Haweswater. The combination of heavy snowfall, light winds and blue sky is – sadly – not a common occurrence in the Lake District.

RIGHT Derwent Island, one of several islands on Derwentwater, is owned by the National Trust and the tenants of its eighteenth-century Italianate mansion travel to and fro by boat. On this occasion, the lake being frozen over, members of Keswick Mountain Rescue had sawn a channel through the ice to enable the tenants (and their dog) to stock up on shopping.

Hoar frost

Hoar frost is especially beautiful to photograph. If there has been a mist and a period of continuously freezing but calm weather, the frost crystals encrusting every surface grow ever larger and take on a magical appearance, not unlike a proper snowfall. Because hoar frost is caused by dampness in the air, it develops more thickly beside water, something we are not exactly short of in the Lake District.

LEFT I can accept the pine needles being so thickly coated with hoar frost, but I was intrigued by each tiny knobble on the fir cone having its very own spike of frost.

BELOW These red berries of the wild guelder rose resemble crystallised fruits with their sugary coating of hoar frost.

LEFT Lanty's Tarn on this exceptionally beautiful New Year's Day was frozen solid and transformed by hoar frost. The original tarn was dammed by the Patterdale Estate to provide ice for Patterdale Hall. On 'Ice Day' a flat-bottomed boat would be placed on the tarn and ice then cut and taken across the dam wall, to be stored in the ice house built into the banking below.

BELOW Ullswater and a frost-coated jetty at Glenridding on an early January morning.

ABOVE Lanty's Tarn, covered by a thick sheet of ice, lies in shadow below this line of birch trees, now properly 'silver'. The photo shows how freezing mist had lain low over the tarn the night before and the freezing damp air had created the white hoar frost. The higher trees on the opposite slope and the mountain in the background remained above the mist, and although still frozen, stayed their normal colour.

RIGHT The view over Ullswater to Place Fell after several days of hard frost.

RIGHT From time to time a tiny stirring of wind caused the hoar frost to waft away in shimmering little clouds. Being at Lanty's Tarn early on this magical New Year's Day morning is an experience I shall always treasure.

BELOW Every inch of every flowing branch on these larch trees at Keldas above Glenridding was decorated with a deep coating of hoar frost on this sparkling morning.

ABOVE This is such a favourite
photo of mine. These hawthorn
twigs look like a witch's fingers,
playing cat's cradle with this
frosty spider's web.

The first of spring

Longer evenings should signal spring and everyone is weary of winter but it is not uncommon for March to bring the very coldest of the winter weather and snow is no surprise, even in April. Sometimes you really have to feel for the daffodils and lambs struggling to stand upright through late snowfalls. On occasions, in a particularly drab period, I have wondered whether the daffodils were actually going backwards, back into the earth. But then the weather relents and very slowly spring catches up. The grass gradually loses its dreary grey-green colour, hazel catkins release clouds of golden pollen and silvery pussy willows shine in the weak sunshine.

RIGHT Rydal Mount was Wordsworth's home for the last thirty-five years of his life and he gave his daughter Dora the little field immediately below the house. After her death Wordsworth planted hundreds of wild daffodils which now fill 'Dora's Field', next to Rydal Church, with a glorious display from the middle of March. I think the overpowering yellow and massing of the larger cultivated daffodils becomes a bit tasteless in the Lake District in spring. They seem to have been planted along so many road verges and roundabouts. But the little native daffodils, especially in woodland, are simple and lovely.

LEFT Mother and lamb.

BELOW Primroses, flowering above the debris of old leaves, are a sure sign of the arrival of spring.

Index

Page numbers refer to captions

In memory of my father, F.F.Poole, from whom I learnt to love the Lakes and take delight in snow.

Acknowledgements

My thanks go, as ever, to my long-suffering tolerant family: my two hugely supportive daughters, Sally and Roz, and, above all, to my tower of strength, my husband Tony. I wish also to praise all those farmers and the work of the many agencies – in particular the National Park and the National Trust – who play such a vital part in protecting our treasured landscape. Without them books like this could not exist.

LEFT The waterfall near the summit of Newlands Pass is just a short walk from the road. It is a spectacular sight when fully frozen.

Frances Lincoln Limited
4 Torriano Mews
Torriano Avenue
London NW5 2RZ
www.franceslincoln.com

Winter in the Lake District
Copyright © Frances Lincoln Limited 2010
Text and photographs copyright © Val Corbett 2010
www.valcorbettphotography.com
First Frances Lincoln edition 2010

A catalogue record for this book is available from the British Library.

978-0-7112-3056-9

Printed and bound in China

1 2 3 4 5 6 7 8 9

Commissioned and edited by Jane Crawley

BELOW This traditional red
phone box on Shap summit
was well known as a centre
for 'cold calling'!